The Chilean Flag

THE CHILEAN FLAG
BY ELVIRA HERNÁNDEZ

TRANSLATED BY ALEC SCHUMACHER
INTRODUCTION BY CECILIA VICUÑA

CHICAGO: KENNING EDITIONS, 2019

INTRODUCTION

In the darkest hour of Chile, Elvira Hernández felt the pain of the symbol:

a little piece of cloth, hurt and wounded, like a human body: the Chilean flag.

La Bandera is an abused woman, an abused symbol.

She has a cunt.

Glorified and abused, the flag is a She.

Elvira Hernández wrote her poem after she herself had been detained and tortured by the dictatorship for not complying with the lies, the ideas now ruling them. Everybody had to obey orders and renounce the right to feel and think, to write as they wished.

The poem itself is tortured, with words distorted and forced to say what the rulers want them to say.

Language could not speak its mind anymore.

Words, like the flag had lost the right to be themselves.

From the perspective of the System, Chileans had to be tortured, because they dared to construct a democratic revolution, acting collectively towards justice, without killing or persecuting opponents. This idea had to be erased from the social body, and they did it by electrocuting indiscriminately the genitals of men and women, to spread Fear far and wide.

While Chileans were trained to look the other way, to go quiet by this terror, Elvira Hernández wrote a poem that could not be printed. Yet, the poem escaped like a prisoner and began circulating in Xeroxes, from hand to hand, until 10 years later it was finally printed in Buenos Aires.

In the poem, each line restores the right of words to speak.

Each word becomes a healer, a prayer for a wounded, enslaved humanity forced to obey the rule of profit over life.

Cecilia Vicuña
New York, October 7, 2018

TRANSLATOR'S PREFACE

I met Elvira Hernández (pen name of María Teresa Adriasola) in 2013 at the café in the Biblioteca Nacional in Santiago while I was conducting research for my doctoral thesis on Chilean poetry of the 1970s and '80s. I came to be interested in her work since I was investigating political poetry and the use of patriotic symbols in literary works. I interviewed her about her most well-known book, *La bandera de Chile*, and asked if she felt there was any connection between her use of the national emblem and the use of the Chilean flags in the work of another contemporary Chilean poet, Juan Luis Martínez. She told me that she remembered being handed a copy of Martínez's *La nueva novela* from her professor, Ronald Kay, in the hallway at university in 1977, opening it up, and seeing the Chilean flag inserted into the book. She said that it was this image that stuck in her mind.

Additionally, I wanted to know what it was like being a student at the time of the military dictatorship. She told me how the universities had been taken over, one had to read in secret places, and that the image of the student was a dangerous figure: if you were walking with a book in hand, you could be stopped and questioned. Writers published their works in small presses, without permission from the censors. And so, *La bandera de Chile*, written in 1981, began to circulate in mimeographed copies in this atmosphere of repression, although it wasn't formally published until 1991 by Libros de Tierra Firme in Buenos Aires.

La bandera de Chile became a symbol of resistance during the dictatorship. It is a testimony, both personal and national, that speaks of physical violation and the lack of agency of marginalized subjects. The Chilean flag takes on a body in the poem, and more specifically, a female body:

The Chilean Flag is hanging from two buildings
her fabric swells up like an ulcerated belly —falls like
an old tit—
like a circus tent
with her legs in the air she has a slit in the middle

The flag is hoisted up and put on display for patriotic festivities, her body exposed, and her volition subjugated. She becomes a symbolic victim, representative of the abuse of power that also includes an abuse of symbols. The flag, as a polyvalent symbol, is able to allude to the violation of the country by the dictatorship as well as the torture, abuse, and sexual violation suffered by victims of political violence. It is significant to note (as Frederico Schopf mentions in his introduction to the 1991 edition of the book) that the poet was detained by the military regime shortly before composing *La bandera de Chile*. Nevertheless, these denunciations of violence are communicated more often by what is not said, since the flag does not speak, but rather "declares her silence".

In Spanish, the Chilean flag is referred to with feminine pronouns (la bandera), but this is because almost all nouns have masculine and feminine pronouns in Spanish. For this reason, it is ambiguous to what degree the Chilean flag is female in the poem, or merely has feminine pronouns related to its linguistic gender. In my translation of *La bandera de Chile*, I wanted to emphasize the way in which the Spanish-language gender of the flag as female coincides with the embodiment of the flag as a female body in the poem. In order to accomplish this, in my first draft I used the feminine pronouns "she", "her", and "hers" in English when referring to the flag, while Daniel Shapiro's translation in *The Oxford Book of Latin American Poetry*, uses the neutral pronouns "it" and "its" for the translated excerpt from Elvira Hernández's work. By using the feminine pronouns, the double meanings of phrases like, "The Chilean flag / is not dedicated to anyone / she surrenders to whomever / knows how to take her" become more apparent to readers unfamiliar with the context of political violence of the Pinochet dictatorship period of Chile.

When I showed my translation to the poet, however, Elvira Hernández responded that she liked the idea of the feminine pronouns but that she wanted to think about it. A few weeks later, I received a cryptic message in which she said that she had dreamed about the Chilean flag and that in her dream she saw that the flag had two faces, one "she" and one "it". So, I returned to the translation, but this time, instead of trying to impose my reading on the poem, I began to search for the two faces of the Chilean flag. I made suggestions to the author for each pronoun based on what she had told me about her dream. For this reason, sometimes the flag is referred to as "she" and sometimes as "it" in this translation. The revision process took longer, but I believe that the result is a much more fascinating text that explores the two faces of the national emblem as well as notions of identity.

The reasons for this translation are many. When I was working as an assistant for Jesse Lee Kercheval (author, translator, and critic), I learned that only about 2-3% of books published in the U.S. are works in translation, and of those, less than a quarter are from female authors. Upon further investigation, I found that very few of the most important Latin American female authors have been translated to English, and since my area of research is contemporary Chilean poetry, I began translating what I felt was the most vital work in need of translation: *La bandera de Chile*.

This book is not only significant in Chilean literature and Latin American literature, but also has an urgent message for readers globally. By poetically exploring the uses and abuses of the national flag in the context of a patriarchal and authoritarian society, readers can come to reflect on the role of patriotism and nationalism as forms of censoring dissident voices and opinions, limiting democratic freedoms. In *La bandera de Chile*, "The Chilean Flag is used as a gag / and that's why surely that's why / no one says anything". Patriotic symbols were used by the military dictatorship to suppress political opposition; thus, the flag becomes a gag. Reflecting on the current rise of nationalism in the West, one can find innumerable examples of enforced patriotism used to silence criticism. In the U.S., a black athlete can lose his/her job and become unhirable by the entire league by refusing to stand for the national anthem. The U.S. National Football League announced on May 23, 2018 that players will be fined if they kneel during the national anthem to protest racial inequality. Additionally, Donald Trump uninvited the 2018 Super Bowl Champion Philadelphia Eagles to the regular White House visit because they failed to respect the national anthem and flag. Instead, on June 5, 2018, he hosted a "Celebration of America" event in honor of the national flag and played the national anthem, saying that those who do not stand for the anthem "shouldn't be in the country." Another poignant example can be seen in Trump's speech on February 5, 2018 in which he called Democrats who didn't applaud him at the State of the Union Address "un-american" and "treasonous". Thus, labeling those who dissent from the dominant ideology as unpatriotic is a rhetorical strategy to denigrate those who disagree, disqualifying them as personae non gratae.

Finally, I would like to mention that I have chosen to translate *La bandera de Chile* with the intent to avoid overt forms of domesticating the text. All translations inevitably suppress some cultural nuances in transferring the sense of the words from one language to another, inscribing the text within domestic cultural values. In order to mitigate this effect, a translator can consciously avoid making the text too easily readable, leaving some of the "foreignness" or defamiliarzing elements in the text by conserving expressions that are not natural in the domestic language. For example, in *La bandera de Chile*, Hernández writes, "Come moscas cuando tiene hambre La Bandera de Chile / en boca cerrada no entran balas", which I have rendered as, "She eats flies when she's hungry The Chilean Flag / in a closed mouth bullets do not enter". The idiomatic expression in Spanish which Hernández is modifying here "en boca cerrada no entran moscas" could be translated more transparently to "the less said, the better". This translation, although easier to comprehend for an English speaker, suppresses the idiosyncrasy of the Spanish expression by replacing it with a parallel idiom. By conserving the Spanish idiom and syntax, the text may seem stranger to an English speaker, but this challenge to common linguistic usage helps remind readers that this is a foreign text, not originally written in English. And since poetic language is often a deviation from linguistic norms (and this book has many deviations from standard expressions), this also coincides with the poetic expression, and conserves the poetry of the text.

Alec Schumacher

THE CHILEAN FLAG

The Chilean flag

    is not dedicated to anyone

she surrenders to whomever

    knows how to take her.

THE TAKING OF THE FLAG

No one has said a word about the Chilean Flag
in its bearing   in the fabric
throughout the entire oblong desert
it has not been named
The Chilean Flag
absent

The Chilean Flag says nothing about herself
she reads herself in her mirror small and round
glinting delayed in time like an echo
there is much broken glass
shattered like the lines of an open hand
read
in search of stones for her desires

A great ignorance aurates the Chilean Flag
it doesn't matter what mother birthed it
honors are professed that centuplicate the infallible
mechanisms
incipient the Chilean Flag there
one hundred two hundred nine hundred
she does not find in others the territory of her own barrens
she does not find in others the fossil of her communal offering
they do not have they do not have spoken even under ragged colors
they do not have they do not have they are not

The Chilean Flag is parted in little flags for the children
and they salute.

                    In other times

the Chilean Flag displays

15% where the star shines for the 10%

displays

whites 20% very pale ones

the Chilean Flag displays in reds The Chilean

                                                  Flag

                    never 100% never

               the 100% of the whole whiblured

                         today

The Chilean Flag is a dwelling said a soldier

and I identify it and unveil it and discover myself

from the Regiment of San Felipe

he said he was dreaming the dwelling better than his barracks

he said he said he said three rooms

hot water shower kitchenette with stove

they applauded like lunatics the dispossessed

The Chilean Flag

Lifts a curtain of smoke the Chilean Flag

asphyxiates and expires not able to do more

                  the flag is incredible

she will never see the burning subsoil of her holy

                               fields

            the lost treasures in the crooks of the air

            the marine burials that are a jewel

we will see the marvelous mountain range sinking in the

                               penumbra

        ficticious she laughs

                    the Chilean Flag

She eats flies when she's hungry The Chilean Flag

in a closed mouth bullets do not enter

she shuts up

high upon the flagstaff

The Chilean Flag is exhibitionist by nature

They send the Chilean Flag up to the top of the flagpole

and that's why she sways and moves her fabric

and that's why they respect it

They hang the Chilean Flag out their windows

they put it on television to solicit tears

nailed to the highest part of a Chilean Empire

on the center flagstaff of the Estadio Nacional

a band passes   a squadron passes

two three four

The Chilean Flag steps out onto the field

in a football match the Chilean Flag is raised

a police cordon surrounds her like at an olympic stadium

(it is all strictly sports)

the Chilean Flag flies through the air

cast to her fate

In meters squared the Chilean Flag is measured
its odor with twitches of the nose
in eyes that do not see her edges of light and dark
in patience her diarrheas
the constructions of malnourished trust

The Chilean Flag is hanging from two buildings
her fabric swells up like an ulcerated belly – falls like
an old tit –

like a circus tent
with her legs in the air she has a slit in the middle
little coochie for the air
a little hole for the ashes of the General O'Higgins
an eye for the Avenida General Bulnes

The Chilean Flag is on her side
forgotten

The Chilean Flag is reversible for
some from here to there
us from there da 'ere

                    The Chilean Flag
                    the perfect division

The Chilean Flag is a foreigner in her own country

        she doesn't have ID

        she isn't majority

        she is no longer recognized

the prolonged fasting has put death's thumb upon her

        the churches administer her last rites

the Legations' party horn and sound of the trumpets

The Chilean Flag forces herself to be more than a flag

No one sees the Chilean Flag passing the nights under the

open sky

the night is dark

not even a long winter it is July 22

—the sun that has made poetry of the solstice—

her children are only asking for the poor part of all of childhood

the Chilean Flag does not have paper for requests

not even a single sheet

nothing at all

Sometimes the Chilean Flag disfarses herself

      a black hood engrievens her visage

      she looks like an executioner of her own colors

no one recognizes her in the puddle where she lives

      if they saw her they don't recall

not even like Vallejo's paletot at full mast

The law is not carried out with the Chilean Flag

she does not have ground beneath her feet

only altitude

The Chilean Flag is in the air

like a paper cone

in the dwelling place of the air that is not aerial

The Chilean Flag asks them not to stand up when she flies

The Chilean Flag with the eye that it has

growing like a star

atheist cyclops

eyeing up and down the edge of changes

fears they may change her name The Chilean Flag

48 hours is the day of the Chilean Flag

       the salutes of hundreds of salvos

       the discourses of fifty sheets of paper

the processions of two or three regiments

the ribbons the standards the banners ad infinitum

       at the speed of light the toasts and honors

The Chilean Flag knows that its day is the day of judgement

Once again the Chilean Flag brandishing daily eczemas

      brings to the table small crumbs leftovers

      the small slivers arrive from poorly slicing thin bread

      to the underside of the Chilean Flag

    thousands of parts of an already shaving of sawdust

   once again the saliva clogged with saliva the Chilean Flag

   again the mouth spits the formless vomitous *chacarilla**

      even though it costs her teeth

---

* "El Acto de Chacarillas" – This was a speech given on July 9, 1977 at a hill named Chacarillas in Santiago where youths gathered for the anniversary of the Frente Juvenil de Unidad Nacional and to commemorate the Battle of La Concepción (1881). Augusto Pinochet presented his "Plan Chacarillas" to the 77 young adults (the number represented the 77 soldiers that died in battle in 1881). The plan established the future of the dictatorship in three stages, including a supposed return to civil governance in 1985. See Cristián Gazmuri, *Historia de Chile: 1891-1994* (RIL editores, 2012).

The yellow of the Old Motherland isn't left in the garret

behind the Chilean Flag's back it plays its grand trick

        with much fanfare and goose-stepping

The museums preserve the story of the Chilean Flag

        dispersed   anonymous   covered up

        the eye can apply its blindness to book

                              frayed

        it's already dead history

The Chilean Flag reposes in a glass case

                (visits during office hours)
                     (pay your dues)

The Chilean Flag escapes down the street swearing to return
        until the death of her death

The battles of the Chilean Flag are losing remembrance

      what was won and lost are fading in the writing

      its flag bearers seem invisible ink

the more Battle of Cancha Rayada is stressed the more surprises

      breaks   mendings   blood stained bandages

      have erased the Chilean Flag from the map

                           crouching

stabbed by matadors' flags she bleeds in a plastic bag

The Chilean Flag is not for sale
        they may cut off her electricity leave her without water
        crush her sides with kicks
the Flag has something of a lure that resists
        the sentences of judges don't matter
        the halyards of aged thread don't matter
The Chilean Flag her limit reached

How dignified the decomposition is devised
                          yes sir! of the Chilean Flag!

                 Whites reds and blues scrambled
                 Pure blue of India en dégradé
          the Chilean Flag en rouge japonais claire

white exile   black standard

How solemnly they leave the lid on the boiling pot
                          yes madame! of the Chilean Flag!

                 The Kansas flag sends her a kiss
                      the Chilean Flag is tired
                  she abandons the custom and melts

```
raise    lower
raise    lower
raise    lower
raise    lower
raise    lower
raise    lower
raise    lower
raise    lower
raise    lower
raise    lower
raise    lower
raise    lower
raise    lower
raise    lower
raise    lower
raise    lower
raise    lower
raise    lower
raise    lower
```

in the routine the Chilean Flag loses heart

and gives in

The Chilean Flag is used as a gag

and that's why surely that's why

no one says anything

The Chilean Flag declares   two points

her silence

LA BANDERA DE CHILE

No se dedica a uno

        la bandera de Chile

se entrega a cualquiera

        que la sepa tomar.

LA TOMA DE LA BANDERA

Nadie ha dicho una palabra sobre la Bandera de Chile

en el porte   en la tela

en todo su desierto cuadrilongo

no la han nombrado

La Bandera de Chile

ausente

La Bandera de Chile no dice nada sobre sí misma

se lee en su espejo de bolsillo redondo

espejea retardada en el tiempo como un eco

hay muchos vidrios rotos

trizados como las líneas de una mano abierta

se lee

en busca de piedras para sus ganas

Una ignorancia padre aurea a la Bandera de Chile

no importa ni madre que la parió

se le rinden honores que centuplean los infalibles

mecanismos

incipiente la Bandera de Chile allí

cien   doscientos   novecientos

no tiene en otros el territorio de sus propios eriazos

no tiene en otros el fósil de su olla común

no tienen no tienen hasta decir so de colores andrajos

no tienen   no tienen   no son

La Bandera de Chile se parte en banderitas para los niños

y saludan.

En otros tiempos

representa la Bandera de Chile

un 15% allí donde brilla la estrella para el 10%

representa

de blancos un 20% de muy pálidos

representa la Bandera de Chile en rojos La Bandera

de Chile

nunca el 100% nunca

el 100% del blanrrozul compacto

hoy

La Bandera de Chile es un pabellón dijo un soldado

y lo identifico y lo descubro y me descubro

del Regimiento de San Felipe

dijo soñaba el pabellón mejor que su barraca

dijo dijo dijo tres dormitorios

ducha de agua caliente cocinilla con horno

aplaudieron como locos los sin techo

La Bandera de Chile

Levanta una cortina de humo la Bandera de Chile

asfixia y da aire a más no poder

es increíble la bandera

no verá nunca el subsuelo encendido de sus campos

santos

los tesoros perdidos en los recodos del aire

los entierros marinos que son joya

veremos la cordillera maravillosa sumiéndose en la

penumbra

ficticia ríe

la Bandera de Chile

Come moscas cuando tiene hambre La Bandera de Chile

en boca cerrada no entran balas

se calla

allá arriba en su mástil

La Bandera de Chile es exhibicionista por naturaleza

A la Bandera de Chile la mandan a la punta de su mástil

y por eso ondea y mueve su tela

y por eso se la respeta

A la Bandera de Chile la tiran por la ventana

la ponen para lágrimas en televisión

clavada en la parte más alta de un Empire Chilean

en el mástil centro del Estadio Nacional

pasa un orfeón   pasa un escalón

dos tres cuatro

La Bandera de Chile sale a la cancha

en una cancha de fútbol se levanta la Bandera de Chile

la rodea un cordón policial como a un estadio olímpíco

(todo es estrictamente deportivo)

La Bandera de Chile vuela por lós aires

echada a su suerte

En metros cuadrados se mide la Bandera de Chile

su olor en respingos de nariz

en ojos que no ven sus aristas de luz y sombra

en paciencia sus diarreas

las construcciones de desnutrida confianza

La Bandera de Chile está tendida entre 2 edificios

se infla su tela como una barriga ulcerada —cae como

teta vieja—

como una carpa de circo

con las piernas al aire tiene una rajita al medio

una chuchita para el aire

un hoyito para las cenizas del General O'Higgins

un ojo para la Avenida General Bulnes

La Bandera de Chile está a un costado

olvidada

La Bandera de Chile es reversible para

    unos de aquí para allá

    sotros edálla pacá

                La Bandera de Chile

                la división perfecta

La Bandera de Chile es extranjera en su propio país
no tiene carta ciudadana
no es mayoría
ya no se la reconoce
los ayunos prolongados le ponen el pulgar de la muerte
las iglesias le ponen la extremaunción
las Legaciones serpentina y sonido de trompetas

La Bandera de Chile fuerza ser más que una bandera

Nadie ve a la Bandera de Chile pasar las noches a la

                                          intemperie

                        la noche es oscura
                 ni que largo invierno es 22 de Julio
              —el sol que ha hecho poesía del solsticio—
          que sus hijos piden sólo la parte pobre de toda la infancia
             la Bandera de Chile no tiene papel para pedidos
                                          ni un pliego
                                          ni nada

A veces se disfarsa la Bandera de Chile

        un capuchón negro le enlutece el rostro

        parece un verdugo de sus propios colores

nadie la identifica en el charco donde vive

        si la han visto no la acuerdan

ni siquiera como el paletó a toda asta de Vallejo

No se cumple la ley con la Bandera de Chile

      no tiene tierra para su pie

          tan sólo altura

La Bandera de Chile está en el aire

                como un cambucho

en la morada del aire que no es aéreo

La Bandera de Chile niega que se pongan de pie a su vuelo

La Bandera de Chile con el ojo que tiene

agrandado como estrella

cíclope ateo

de arriba abajo mirando el filo de los cambios

teme le cambien el nombre La Bandera de Chile

De 48 horas es el día de la Bandera de Chile
       los saludos de centenas de salvas
       de cincuenta carillas los discursos
de dos y tres regimientos las procesiones
las escarapelas los estandartes los pendones al infinito
       a la velocidad de la luz los brindis y honores

La Bandera de Chile sabe que su día es el del juicio

De nuevo la Bandera de Chile enarbolando eczemas diarias

trae a colación pocas migas que sobran de la mesa

el menuzo llega de quien mal parte el pan menudo

al envés de la Bandera de Chile

milésimas partes de ya un aserrín onzavo

de nuevo la saliva atorada de saliva la Bandera de Chile

de nuevo la boca escupe la chacarilla vomitosa sin especie

aunque le cueste los dientes

No se queda en el desván el amarillo de la Patria Vieja

que a espaldas de la Bandera de Chile hace su gran juego

a mucho paso de ganso

Los museos guardan la historia de la Bandera de Chile
disuelta   anónima   encubierta
el ojo puede aplicar su ceguera por libro
deshilachada

es historia ya muerta

La Bandera de Chile reposa en estuche de vidrio

(visitas en horas de oficina)
(cancele su valor)

La Bandera de Chile escapa a la calle y jura volver
hasta la muerte de su muerte

Pierden sus anuarios los combates de la Bandera de Chile
      lo ganado y lo perdido lo pierden en la letra
      parecen de tinta invisible sus abanderados
más Cancha Rayada se subraya más de sorpresas
       roturas   remiendos   sangre salpicada de parches
      han borrado del map a la Bandera de Chile
                     en cuclillas
banderilleada piede sangre en una carpa de plástico

La Bandera de Chile no se vende

      le corten la luz la dejen sin agua

      le machuquen los costados a patadas

La Bandera tiene algo de señuelo que resiste

      no valen las sentencias de los jueces

      no valen las drizas de hilo curado

La Bandera de Chile al tope

¡Con qué dignidad se cuece la descomposición
                    ¡sí señor! de la Bandera de Chile!

                Blancos rojos y los azules revueltos
                Puro azul de la India en degradé
            la Bandera de Chile en rouge japonais claire

blanco exilio   pendón negro

¡Con qué seriedad no se destapa la olla
                    ¡sí señora! de la Bandera de Chile!

                La bandera de Kansas le manda un besito
                    se cansa la Bandera de Chile
                    deja la tradición y se derrite

izar	arriar
izar	arriar
izar	arriar
izar	arriar
izar	arriar
izar	arriar
izar	arriar
izar	arriar
izar	arriar
izar	arriar
izar	arriar
izar	arriar
izar	arriar
izar	arriar
izar	arriar
izar	arriar
izar	arriar
izar	arriar
izar	arriar

en la rutina la Bandera de Chile pierde su corazón

y se rinde

La Bandera de Chile es usada de mordaza

y por eso seguramente por eso

nadie dice nada

La Bandera de Chile declara   dos puntos

su silencio

ELVIRA HERNÁNDEZ (Lebu, Chile, 1951), seudonym of María Teresa Adriasola, is a Chilean poet, essayist, and literary critic. She is one of the most important voices of contemporary poetry in the Southern Cone and the Chilean neo-avant-garde (also known as the Escena de avanzada) although she eschews such categorical markers. Some of her most important works include: *¡Arre! Halley ¡Arre!* (1986), *Meditaciones físicas por un hombre que se fue* (1987), *Carta de Viaje* (1989), *La bandera de Chile* (1991), *El orden de los días* (1991), *Santiago Waria* (1992), *Álbum de Valparaíso* (2002), *Cultivo de hojas* (2007), *Cuaderno de deportes* (2010), *Actas urbe* (2016) and *Pájaros desde mi ventana* (2018). Recently she was the recipient of the Jorge Tellier National Poetry Award (2018) and the Pablo Neruda Ibero-American Poetry Award (2018).

ALEC SCHUMACHER (Green Bay, 1983) received his Ph.D. from the University of Wisconsin-Madison (2017) and is currently Assistant Professor of Spanish at Gonzaga University. His research focus is Chilean poetry of the neo-avant-garde, in particular, Juan Luis Martínez and Elvira Hernández. He has translated poetry by Jorge Arbeleche in *Drunken Boat Press* and poems by Elvira Hernández in *Asymptote* and *Make Literary Magazine*.

CECILIA VICUÑA is a poet, artist, filmmaker and activist, addressing ecological destruction, human rights and cultural homogenization. The author of 22 poetry books, her *New & Selected Poems of Cecilia Vicuña* is from Kelsey Street Press, 2018.

ISBN: 978-0-9997198-6-2
Library of Congress Control Number: 2019931661

Cover design by Julietta Cheung

Published by Kenning Editions in Chicago, IL
3147 W Logan Blvd, Ste 7, Chicago, IL 60647

Kenningeditions.com

Distributed by Small Press Distribution
1341 Seventh St., Berkeley, CA 94710

Spdbooks.org

This book was made possible in part by the supporters of
Kenning Editions: Charles Bernstein, Julietta Cheung, Joel
Craig, Craig Dworkin, Jais Gossman, Judith Goldman, Rob
Halpern, Lyn Hejinian, Joshua Hoglund, Brenda Iijima,
Kevin Killian, Rodney Koeneke, Adalaide Morris, Caroline
Picard, Barbara Troolin, Anna Vitale, and Tyrone Williams.

Kenning Editions is a 501c3 non-profit, independent literary
publisher investigating the relationships of aesthetic quality
to political commitment. Consider donating or subscribing:
Kenningeditions.com/shop/donation